sundance
LITTLE BLUE
READERS

Making Lemonade

Focus: Designing, Making and Appraising
Systems

PETER SLOAN &
SHERYL SLOAN

- Get six to eight large ripe lemons.
- Get a cup of sugar or sweetener.
- Get a jug, a knife, a lemon squeezer, a large spoon, and a cutting board.

- Ask an adult to help you cut the lemons into halves.
- Use a cutting board under the knife.

- Set one piece of lemon aside.
- Squeeze the rest of the lemons on the squeezer.
- Pour the juice into the jug.

- Fill two thirds of the jug
  with water and add
  most of the sugar.
- Stir the water, sugar,
  and the juice with
  the spoon.
- Keep stirring until all
  the sugar is dissolved.

- Taste the mixture.
- If it is too sour, add more sugar.
- If it is too sweet, add more water and stir.

- Put some ice cubes into your lemonade.
- Cut up the leftover piece of lemon and put the lemon slices into the jug.

- Now your lemonade is ready to drink.
- Keep your leftover lemonade in the refrigerator.

Stage 1
1. Machines in the Home
2. Making a Car
3. Tools at Home
4. Floating
5. The Class Newspaper
6. From Grass to Milk
7. My Boat
8. Growing Beans

Stage 2
1. Using Machines
2. Electricity at Work
3. Parts of a Bike
4. Signs Everywhere
5. Sharing Time
6. Garbage Day
7. Baking a Cake
8. Front Loader

Stage 3
1. Flying Machines
2. Rain
3. Trains
4. Using Fire
5. Wheels at Work
6. Big Machines
7. Making Lemonade
8. Fences and Walls

Stage 4
1. Computers
2. Gasoline for the Car
3. Electric Motors
4. Making a Plane
5. Ships and Boats
6. Old and New Trains
7. Making a Tape
8. What If...?

Stage 5
1. Water for You
2. Making Electricity
3. Making an Ooze Monster
4. Machines in the School
5. Build It Big
6. Instruments
7. The Hospital
8. Machines on the Farm

sundance
LITTLE BLUE
READERS

Little Blue Readers—the next generation in the *Sundance family of books for emergent readers.*

Little Blue Readers begin at the emergent level for children ready for nonfiction. These books feature stunning photography with engaging, informational text. In fact, they are an early introduction to information reference books. **Little Blue Readers** are graded and keyed at every level to the following content strands:

Designing, Making and Appraising
Information
Materials
Systems

Teachers will find wide application for **Little Blue Readers** in the daily science and social studies work in their classroom. Children will enjoy the success of being able to read real "big kids" information written at their own reading level.

S T A G E
1 2 3 4 5

ISBN 0-7608-3174-2

9 780760 831748

Reproductive Rights
and Reproductive Health:

A Concise Report

United Nations